Perspectives of Nature

Volume 4

Perspectives of Nature Volume 4
ISBN (print book): 978-1-955762-10-6
ISBN (ebook): 978-1-955762-11-3

Published by
The Shy Writer
www.theshywriter.org

Cover art by:
Owen Košir
Taken at Myrick Park in Wisconsin

Perspectives of Nature Volume 4

Scientifically Romantic and Experiential Nature Poetry

by: Paul Košir

ACKNOWLEDGEMENTS

I must gratefully acknowledge
Rodney Schroeter,
whose confidence from the beginning
in my scientifically romantic style of poetry
made this project imaginable
and whose advice during the process
made the project achievable.

I also must gratefully acknowledge
the contributions to this work
of the members of our
Wednesday Night Poets Group,
who helped me to polish my good poems
into publishable works.

Finally, I must gratefully acknowledge
my wife, Lilly, and our son, Owen,
for their cheerful and helpful responses
to my frequent questions and complaints
while dealing ineffectively
with computer situations.

Author's Introduction

For more than two decades, I wrote no poems.

This followed my initial burst of nearly a dozen poems beginning in the late 1980s, when I wrote poetry that described the science behind natural phenomena and processes. It was picturesque, instructive, and sometimes lighthearted. Early in 2012, I emerged from my dormancy with "Sun Dogs," a poem that appears in my first collection, *Perspectives of Nature*. I wrote that book, in part, to see if I still had the knack for writing poetry after time off as a father, teacher, naturalist, and historian. The result was that I developed a truly unique style that I called "Scientifically Romantic".

The poems I wrote were scientifically accurate, yet full of wonderment.

I became confident in my abilities and in this new style and published two more books of poetry: *Perspectives of Nature Volume 2,* with fewer meteorological and astronomical poems, and *Perspectives of Nature Volume 3,* with more "story" poems, a trend also found in *Volume 2.*

Although more philosophical at times, the fourth volume of *Perspectives of Nature* is still, at heart, a collection of poems that accurately describe the natural world without romanticizing it, yet encourages personal feeling, a trademark of the Romantic Movement in poetry.

William Wordsworth, a founder of the Romantic Movement, said, "poetry is the spontaneous overflow of powerful feelings."

May you have many 'Wordsworthian' moments as you read the poetry in *Perspectives of Nature Volume 4.*

Many of the poems in this booklet use scientific terms. Definitions of more obscure terms and less-frequently-used words can be found on the left-hand page opposite the poem in which the words or terms occur.

Readers may want to use the blank portions of the left-hand pages for journal entries, recording when and where events described in the poems are observed. Seeing a light pillar or the Milky Way, experiencing a mayfly hatch, or even finding a cowbird egg in a nest, are all worthy of journal entries.

Writing in this book would not mar its pages, but cause them to flower.

-- P. K.
May, 2022

To Lilly,

who's always been supportive wife
in my not-always-normal life.

Table of Contents

FEEDING BISON

The herd was tens of millions strong when money changed no hands,
yet currency of bison skins brought more and more demands.

Once ev'rywhere but near the coasts, no thought they'd disappear.
Then slaughter inconceivable, two million in a year.

When dozens left in Yellowstone created public fears.
No longer being targeted helped dry the public's tears.

Restrictive hunting laws enforced, the bison bred like deer,
Now herd is half-a-million head, their comeback makes us cheer.

We drove all day on family trip in station wagon car;
no phones or tunes or videos, the drive seemed very far.

We missed by minutes open hours to see the bison park.
With silver tongue, Dad made a deal that wouldn't miss the mark.

We'd ride along with staff and feed the bison herd a snack
with Mom in middle, Dad on right, and children in the back.

A worker drove us in his truck to middle of the herd.
"Don't touch the horns!" he sternly warned two times and then a third.

Its head as big as all of me, I feared for being bit,
but there, inside the pickup truck, I didn't want to quit.

Such herbivores ate only grass, so it would do no harm.
Yet when I fed it pellet food, it sucked up half my arm.

Nyger *(NYE-jer)*
   The trademarked name held by the Wild Bird
   Feeding Institute for the seeds of the niger, a
   yellow daisy native to Africa with seeds similar
   to those of thistles.

GOLDFINCHES

My father never liked to change; he gladly lived in ruts,

but knew he should not miss a chance before a doorway shuts.

A thrifty man, within his means was how he lived his life,

was always thrilled with gifts received, best of all, from wife.

She knew always what he wanted (a thought before he did):

a modest gift, complete with task for her to keep it hid.

He couldn't wait to open up the presents that she bought,

not socks, nor ties, nor underwear, nor other things he sought.

That year my mother's gift for him and thistle-eating birds,

a feeder finches would enjoy, but not our squirrel herds.

My father set it up anon, along with Nyger fill.

That day two finches stopped to eat and gave us all a thrill.

Dad pondered the supplies on hand, a twinkle in his eye;

he had enough materials, to make a test to try.

Next day he went to hardware store to buy more things he'd need

to make the feeding stations for the fourteen birds we'd feed.

Scutes *(skoots)* or *(skyoots)*
    Horny or bony plates covering a turtle's shell.

TURTLE SHELLS

A turtle with no shell attached would not a turtle be.
Its shell encumbers not its life, but neither sets it free.
Protective plates upon its back, reduced mobility,
adaptation set the course for shell anatomy.

Its scutes as plates of armor serve to shield and thus defend
both body and the skin beneath, on which the scutes depend.

The upper shell, or carapace, makes turtles look distinct
while plastron, or the lower shell, by flesh and bone is linked.

Box turtle species have a "hinge" across the bottom shell
affording them a little "box" in which they fit quite well.

By pulling in all legs and head, they hide from predators;
then pressing plastron, carapace, will open up its "doors".

The Blanding's turtle (semi-box) has "hinge" that's used in fear
to cover head and legs in front, but not the ones in rear.

An adaptation found in some freshwater-dwelling kinds
is soft shell with consistency of firmest citrus rinds.

The Swinhoe's softshell, rare on Earth, can live a hundred years;
so nearly all were hunted out, now real extinction fears.
A male lives in captivity, a female, Viet Nam.
These two must be together bred so she can be a mom.

CCC (Civilian Conservation Corps)
  A government program which, along with
  The Works Progress Administration (WPA)
  provided jobs for young men during the
  1930s at work camps like the one in Wyalusing.

Caterpillar® tread
  Track of large earth-moving equipment.

SHELTER

With our country at its poorest,
some young men made it rich;

they built us timeless treasures while
in governmental hitch.

In Wyalusing, shelters rose
at hands of CCC.

Though built for humans, used by bats,
without an entrance fee.

Bats congregate 'neath roofing boards
and squeak like mice on high.

They face adapted predator
that doesn't even fly.

A black rat snake can use its scutes
as Caterpillar® tread

to climb the rough-hewn timbers where
on bats itself is fed.

Notes

COWBIRD AND MINK

In a hole in a tree, on a twig in a nest,
cowbird laid a speckled egg after mother laid the rest.

The last to be produced, yet still the first to hatch,
it was biggest in the nest and the bully of the batch.

Always food for cowbird, yet rarely for her own,
the mother knew her duty, feed all nestlings until grown.

Brood now left in hardship, with offspring yet to fledge,
when predator came closer to a tree along the edge.

Up a tree, in a hole, mink cornered little meal;
now birds were unprotected and the mammal, poised to steal.

Pressing in still deeper, its space becoming tight,
the mink was quite immobile as the dawn broke morning light.

From a hole in a tree, on a twig in a nest,
we flung the unharmed body of each uninvited guest.

Dapple
    Become marked with rounded
    patches of color or light.

Troll
    To fish from a slowly moving boat
    or other craft.

Ice floe
    A floating chunk of ice in a river.

BIRTHDAY PRESENTS

My wife enjoys her birthday date,
it always falls in March.

She never asks for birthday cake
with sweeteners or starch.

She likes instead to go outside,
clear weather, rain, or snow

to dapple in the sunny spots
along the river's flow.

Her greatest thrill is eagles seen,
in air, on ice, or nest,

or trolling from an ice floe chunk
that gives birds' wings a rest.

This burst of Life at Winter's close,
when eagles congregate,

one hundred thirty numbered once
and made her celebrate.

Lepidoptera
    The taxonomic order lepidoptera comprises
    the butterflies, skippers, and moths.

Blue Butterflies
    The rarest Blue Butterfly is the Miami Blue,
    of which less than one hundred remain (all
    on the first two Florida Keys).
    The next rarest is the Karner Blue,
    of which 90% live in Wisconsin.

BUTTERFLY PARK

My sister took me to a zoo of speciality.
No mammals, birds, or fishes there for visitors to see,

just skippers, moths, and butterflies, the lepidoptera,
from tropics and the temp'rate lands near southern Florida.

I walked into enclosure huge, took third step then aback.
"Was that a reddish arc I saw on forewings brown and black?"

With many thousand butterflies from Tropics in the room,
I saw Red Admiral Butterfly on tiny Nettle bloom.

My seeing butterfly I knew, spurred me to look for more,
for reading all the species signs seemed like a mammoth chore.

By looking for the common ones, I thought I'd better fare;
With only time for quickest glance, I'd have no time to stare.

A Comma or a Question Mark? I wasn't really sure.
Those butterflies look much alike, distinctions sometimes blur.

The Swallowtails were largest there; Blue butterflies were least.
Their rarest cousin was not there; its habitat decreased.

My eyes grew larger, most impressed by being in a zoo
where butterflies exalted were and common given due.

The peregrine falcon was officially
listed as endangered from 1973 to 1999.

NEIGHBORHOOD BIRDS

My sister lived in Florida, in southern part of state,
Directly 'cross the tollway from community with gate.

We drove around to see inside what was so very good;
Nice cars and houses, that was all, in fancy neighborhood.

Back at my sister's place, perhaps, were nature sights for me,
like lizards running hither, yon, or birds I'd rarely see.

Then, happy day, black vulture high, and hawk upon her house,
the once-endangered peregrine was diving on a mouse.

Compleat

An archaic form of the word complete that
includes the notion of having all necessary or
desired aspects of something, as is the case in
The Compleat Angler by Isaak Walton,
first published in 1653.

16

MAY FLIES

Other species have a "hatch," but none is quite so grand
as that made by Ephemera, the largest in the land.

So big in fact, emergence seen by RADAR, set for rain,
a tool now used by scientists to watch swarms grow and wane.

Four 'flies bounced off my flailing arms, one hit me in the ear,
a few alighted on each leg, a dozen flew too near.

Such living clouds appear at dusk and congregate near light,
lay waste upon a river town, may stay till dark of night.

The swarm begins near water source, that's clean enough to "hatch"
a thousand million mayfly duns, enormous breeding batch.

Drab duns become more colorful as they to spinners change,
this second adult insect stage, unique and rather strange.

With no reserves, she lays her eggs from surface, on her back;
eggs gently sink, adhere to logs, or fall to bottom black.

Those eggs transform to naiads (nymphs) one time or manyfold;
the nymphs live then at least a year, this life is rarely told.

A day or two live adult males then go on land to die,
while females live a shorter span, she mates while in the sky.

Their mouth parts rudimentary, adults don't bite or eat,
when larval nymphs eat food enough, life cycle is compleat.

While laying eggs, the mayflies are like "sitting ducks" for fish,
who easily can eat their fill of tasty insect dish.

Fly fishers tie their flies to look like mayflies to a trout
then act as insects in a swarm to catch a fish to tout.

Notes

Caste
A grouping of social insects all of which
have the same function in the colony.

High Hopes
The 1959 song made popular by
Frank Sinatra about attempts by an ant
to move a rubber tree plant.

LEAFCUTTER ANTS

Some thousands of chambers for queen and her kin,
but only her daughters will live there within.

From dozens to millions, a colony holds
the ants for all jobs in production of molds:

cut leaves while they're green, store in beds underground,
make mulch for the fungus to which they are bound.

The labor's divided by size for each caste,
the soldiers are largest, while farmers are last.

Crop-growers, as smallest, take care of the young;
they vaccinate larvae and take out the dung.

The larger ants sometimes will help clear a trail
if an object too big and smaller ants fail.

With leaf-cutting roles so ingrained in the ants,
someday they'd be movers of rubber tree plants,

but slippery leaves with which no insect copes,
means ant could not move them, whatever her hopes.

Ruse *(rooz)*
    A stratagem or trick

Feign *(fane)*
    To pretend to be affected by something

Ploy
    A stratagem or cunning maneuver

Coy
    Shy, retiring, or pretending to be same

Plover *(PLUH - ver* or *PLOH - ver)*
    A small wading bird

Apportioning
    Dividing out into portions

KILLDEER

While jogging 'long the Oakwood Road, a rural city street
in the County of Milwaukee, where Nature, suburb meet,

    I saw a bird just sitting there, in shoulder of the lane.
    It sat until I got too near and triggered ruse to feign.

With open nest upon the ground, it made a daring ploy,
it limped away with 'broken' wing, behavior never coy.

    Rejuvenated from its 'wound,' it ran in fits and starts,
    apportioning its getaway in many shorter parts.

    It led me as a 'predator' with thoughts of easy meal
until the plover flew away, squawked "killdeer" then, with zeal.

The next day, for my morning jog, I chose the other way
to give protective parent rest while at its nest could stay.

    I looked not back, for I had seen behavior at its best,
to guard the eggs or nestlings that were camouflaged like nest.

I knew I'd miss the chance to see that bird repeat its trick,
but rather give best chance at life to each and every chick.

Forb
    A wild, flowering plant.

A SURPRISE

Toward colors of the forb I crept, to photograph the bloom
with flowers' petals woven low in Mother Nature's loom.

For land ne'er touched by human hands, nor sprinkler, nor mower,
I wanted level nature shot, so knelt down even lower.

But when too close to Earth I leaned, a milk snake buzzed its tail
in driest leaves to scare me off. In that it did not fail.

I knew it was not rattlesnake, but that was just my smarts.
I yelped and fled from unseen snake as told by heart of hearts.

Badger Camper
>One who attends Wisconsin Badger Camp,
a recreational camp for persons of all abilities.

Hale
>Strong and healthy; hearty.

ANOTHER SURPRISE

Each week I'd lead a hike or two or three
at camp for those with disability.

The Badger Campers followed me on trail,
we slowed the pace if someone was not hale.

I stopped the hike when something made a sound.
Could not mistake this rattle from the ground.

"We must go back. A big tree blocks our way,"
a counsellor, quick-witted, thought to say.

This cleared the path before the snake could strike.
Without that snake, we finished off our hike.

Notes

CUCKOO

I'd never seen a cuckoo,
the European kind,
but led a German walker
and had to change his mind.
The bird walk went to boat launch,
I saw a cuckoo's nest.
The walker said, "You're crazy,
unless, of course, you jest."
I, "Cuckoos in *our* country,
black-billed and yellow, too,
will build nests that look shabby,
which *your* birds never do.
Our species like your cuckoo,
that doesn't build a nest,
is named 'brown-headed cowbird,'
with nestlings never blest."

Crni Lug (*TSER-nee loog*)
   A village (pop. 250) in Gorski Kotar
   (Mountainous Region) of Croatia.

Wiles
   Cunning maneuvers or procedures

CUCKOO TOO

Hitched a ride to Crni Lug.
Too dark to street signs see.
Wandered 'round, afraid to knock.
Where could my friend's house be?
Slept behind the church that night
on stack of roofing tiles.
Tried to find some comfort there
while gathering my wiles.
The night was cool and quiet.
Lodged there until the dew.
Crickets kept me stark awake
till called a bird "Cuckoo."

Notes

HIGH WAY C

Owl

One day in sunny morning-time, I walked on highway near,
to get my daily exercise, and see some birds I'd hear.

Identifying singing birds was one of my great joys,
but on that day, so many birds, their songs were background noise.

Then, suddenly, though in the day, a barred owl made a hoot.
As dominoes, birds dropped their songs till every one was mute.

The silence broken, thereupon, each bird gave sharpest call,
communicating hawk or owl, to warn birds one and all.

Wild Turkeys

Another walk on Highway C
produced a splendid sight to see.

Impossible ten years before,
a view of turkeys, more and more.

Reintroduced Missouri stocks,
split up to form Wisconsin flocks.

The birds became good residents,
with hunts where population dense.

That day the turkeys, one by one,
flew 'cross the road till thirty done.

Crepuscular
Active in the twilight hours of dawn and dusk.

Hiawatha
The Hiawatha *(high-uh-WAH-thuh)* National
Forest is in the Upper Peninsula of Michigan.

PORCUPINE

Each year we count our breeding birds
to note the rise or fall

of numbers in their habitats
and help when they get small.

To Hiawatha first we went,
where counters were before,

to chart how data changed from past,
the science not a chore.

Arising much more difficult
at quarter after four.

Then we saw life crepuscular,
a porcupine afore.

I rushed to pet the animal,
just missed the needled beast.

I tried to show bravado,
but pet attempt was least.

The Seney *(SEE-nee)* National Wildlife Refuge
is in the Upper Peninsula of Michigan.

OTTERS

Our survey done, the count complete,

we wanted next a little treat.

More wildlife seen in refuge near

might fill our eyes and give us cheer.

We therefore changed our pathway back

and took the Seney Refuge track.

Indeed, we saw in open pond

what made us smile with feelings fond:

a raft of otters set to play

by treading water in the bay.

They looked like people in a pool.

Do people look like otters? Cool.

Notes

Fern species
   The two fern species highlighted in this poem
   are the Bulblet Fern and the Walking Fern.

Strown
   (Past participle of strow,
   the archaic form of strew.)
   Scattered or spread about.

FERNS

I took a stroll on shady bluff between two types of ferns,
while one could follow any path, one only downward turns.

Each species reproduced itself by spores and not by seeds,
so cloaked the cliff with lacy green, not flower-colored weeds.

Though tiny, spores hold DNA instructions for the plant.
Spores moist and sheltered, germinate, but otherwise they can't.

Two generations alternate; the "fern", or sporophyte,
and overlooked gametophyte, a fingernail in height.

The ferns along the trail I trod regenerated there,
without the spores of other ferns nor reproductive pair.

Ferns do it vegetatively, each bulb is then a clone,
a tiny bulb along plant's keel, by Mother Nature strown.

Dried bulblets move by gravity, along the bluff-side edge
until they meet an obstacle, stopped by a little ledge.

The other fern can 'walk' the Earth, re-rooting forms its 'grip',
then takes a step, a growing stride, re-roots again at tip.

Moot
    Open to discussion, but of no significance.

Generative
    Growing into a new plant, as, the fruits.

FRUITS

It cannot be, you must be wrong!
I'll show you books. It won't take long.

It sounds not right. How can it be?
Come take a look. Let's have a see.

That's not the story I've been told.
As scientists, we must be bold.

The question is no longer moot?
Tomatoes are a type of fruit!

Is it the only food like that?
When fruit puts on a veggie's hat?

And takes the culinary name?
Even when it's not the same?
So many fruits from ovaries,
like peppers, olives, okra, peas,

still considered vegetative,
even though parts generative.

What rhubarb parts meet baking goals?
The stalks of leaves, or petioles.

Whatever fruity taste belief?
Not fruit, but stems of each large leaf.

Replaces fruit by those who bake,
and pinch off buds to crumbles make.

This sour produce just may be
what goes down hard *for you and me.*

Wants for
  Needs

Food
  Nutrients

To bite
  To be made available for chemical reaction

Aground
  On the ground

Foil
  That which enhances the qualities of another
  by contrast.

OAKS and MAPLES

A maple's almost only tree that in its shade can grow,
while oaks in shade of any tree have growth that's rather slow.

So maple woods are deep and dim with mostly maple trees,
yet here and there a basswood tree gives pollen used by bees.

The oak woods bright and open are, competitors abound.
Black oaks prefer the drier sites, few species there are found.

When maples lose their leaves in Fall, their foliage is bright.
That matters not in Nature's eyes, She wants for food to bite.

October maple leaves aground are good, so rarely seen
for Decomposers on the spot can pick the leaf stems clean.

Yet oaks hold tight their leaves to get the last nutrition bits
until November, some trees March, before their leaf-fall quits.

The maples more nutrition lose; it's in the leaves they drop.
Since maples grow in their own shade, those trees come out on top.

The oaks are much more frugal of nutrition in the soil,
October leaves less nutritive, oaks are the maples' foil.

Stomates (also stomata)
Minute pores in the surfaces of leaves
that allow gas exchange.

EVERGREENS

In Winter, when the broad-leaved trees
are dried by Nature's frozen breeze,
leaves fall to Earth, where they will die,
but not from cold, just much too dry.
With waxy coat and needle shape
and stomates rarely held agape,
a pine survives the winter bleak
with moisture never more than meek.
All pines, like broad-leaved trees, will lose
the leaves that act on Autumn's cues.
Half the needles fall each year
from white pines, leaving browse for deer.
By species certain portions fall:
a third, a fourth, a fifth, or all.
The last is larch or tamarack,
its late-year needles pigments lack.
The first four show, with winter green,
the life in death by Faith that's seen.

Notes

CLIMBING TREES

When young, I used to climb the trees in our one-acre yard.
The larger trees had trunks mature, which made the climbing hard.
The rules I used for climbing trees is why I never fell.
The wisdom of these guiding words applied to life as well.
When lighting first begins to dim, go not too far out on a limb.
Use always three points of support: self, knowledge, God of any sort.

While on a trip
to trees Northwest,
where rainfall helps
them grow their best,
I left my climbing
days behind,
no longer feeling
so inclined.
Because the trees
were much too tall,
without the skills,
I'd likely fall.
No ropes, no spurs
were ever tried.
I climbed enough
to rest inside,
within the strength
of sturdy tree,
so safe, secure,
it let me be.

Sallying
    The hunting technique in which
    birds fly out from a branch,
    nab an insect out of the air,
    and return to the branch,
    also called hawking.

WHO SAID I DIDN'T GO

The air was fresh, the breezes light,
the grass had dotted dew.

The Sun began to warm the Earth,
the sky turned brilliant blue.

While hiking we saw many birds,
I named each one in turn.

The songs and calls of birds we saw
were next for them to learn.

I noted bill diversity
that matched the way they ate:

a cone-shaped cracker, sipping straw,
and chisel for a trait.

Two rivals hunted same resource,
each living by its tally.

The swallows caught bugs on the wing,
the pewees caught by sally.

With unlike feeding styles, the birds
stayed out of other's way.

They taught us how they share the wealth
while eating insect prey.

We saw more birds that blessed hike
and heard a Sunday crow.

When hikers talked of church, one said,
"Who said I didn't go?"

Notes

USING TIME

The never-ending currency
of Time well-spent today

will ne'er be lost, but always found,
whatever come what may.

Struck only once by hands of Time,
but minted every day

and crafted into food and drink,
exchanging weigh for whey.

Our recompense for daily toil
is promise of more work,

until we cease our labors there
our duties for to shirk.

The gold we've sought through our careers
cannot be held in hand,

but choices that at last we make
based solely on the Land.

Notes

SKIPPING STONES

I learned to skip stones flat and smooth
from older, smarter cousin,

but even with his tutelage,
I couldn't bounce a dozen.

My cousin, Don, skipped other things,
whatever shape they'd take.

A marble once he even threw,
and made it skim the lake.

I tried not many times and thought,
"With round I'll not excel."

I tried again with flatter stones,
but didn't do as well.

All week we pitched stones in the drink,
his numbers out of reach,

so next time we were at the lake,
we simply walked the beach.

Notes

LIFE

A beating heart begins from start,
the mind unstraps with missing gaps
that parents fill with unused frill
as children wait to see their fate.

While Nature's led by Father Time,
He lets Her live and learn,
but when they part their ended ways,
no Future to discern.

Notes

LEARNING NATURE

How happy is the learner who, in Time, becomes aware
that forms of Life, while similar, if common or if rare,

can be distinguished from the rest, to show diversity,
as in the ferns, the clams, and frogs and small arrays we see.

This revelation sparks the mind to know some varied types,
but not enough to master groups with many diff'rent stripes.

The study of the larger sets, like fishes, birds, and trees
is slow at first, till tipping point, then learning has more ease.

Beyond the tipping point, some know the Life that can be found,
if over, under, on the Earth, it serves as common ground.

Enormous groups still harder seem, the insects and the plants.
They're often left to experts and their sub-specific rants.

Karst landscape
Landscape characterized by the dissolving
of rock to form features like caves, sinkholes,
and springs.

Clave
Past tense of cleave.

ICE CAVE

A cave in northeast Iowa, formed just like all the rest,
helped make the corner of that state karst landscape ever blest.

The water found inside the Earth became an acid weak,
dissolving limestone, dolomite at concentration peak.

Time carved the caverns found within this ordinary cave,
whose passage follows fracture lines that Mother Nature clave.

Thus, air impounded underground is insulated well,
it's steady near the average, thermometer can tell.

Yet ice cave found in Iowa entraps the coldest air,
which circulates around its rooms so cold is everywhere.

No reason found can yet explain why ice coats walls inside,
how air can always frozen feel at entrance open wide.

In largest cave from Badlands east where cavers see their breaths,
if normal cave life tried it there, they soon would meet their deaths.

We know the reasons Earth is warm and getting warmer soon,
yet no one's sure why cave is cold in latter parts of June.

Ablate
> Waste away or erode a glacier,
> iceberg, or rock by the melting of ice
> or the action of water.

Canyon Grand
> The Grand Canyon in Arizona.

Arches
> Arches National Park in Utah.

EROSION

With a steady, infinitesimal gait,

Time does all His work at a slow, even rate.

The persistence of Time will never abate,

even when frozen, will the surface ablate.

Time-honored erosion, need not mediate,

the work is unending, to disintegrate.

Time sharpens His tools for eroding the land,

but tools in His kit are not built for the hand.

They have not a case nor an imprint nor brand.

With wind and some water, He beats earth to sand.

In two blinks of His eye, He dug Canyon Grand,

honed parabola Arches in rusty red band.

Cirrus clouds
    Wispy clouds made of ice crystals.

Illusory *(ill-OO-zaw-ree)*
    Not real, as an illusion.

LIGHT PILLARS

Ice crystals from low cirrus clouds,
suspended in the air,

with position horizontal,
cause pillars that are rare.

The crystals act as mirrors do,
reflecting nearby light,

arrangement rather vertical,
they form a shaft that's bright.

If shaft arises near the Sun
according to our view,

we say "solar" or "sun" pillars
with sunset-colored hue.

If columns other lights adorn,
like street-lamps or the Moon,

we use not solar epithet
for pillars that formed soon,

right after sunset, cold and still,
or ere the next sunrise.

But pedestal illusory,
'tis only in our eyes.

Hera *(HAIR-uh)*
   The Greek goddess Hera
   was renamed Juno by the Romans.

Heracles *(HAIR-uh-klees)*
   The Greek hero Heracles
   was renamed Hercules by the Romans.

MILKY WAY

Our galaxy was named by Greeks from legendary tale,
when Hera, nursing Heracles lost milk in glowing trail.

Astronomers in ancient times, as Hera felt dismay,
looked up to hazy patch in sky and named it "Milky Way."

They saw not hundred billion lights nor spiral arms nor bars.
From Earth, can't see Way's blackest hole, just forests of its stars.

The nearby stars as trees are seen, some up, some down, ahead.
For distant stars, not each is seen, galactic glow instead.

The far-off trees give edge-on view, green stripe upon the land.
In darkened skies on cloudless nights, the galaxy's a band.

While pondering black holes and Time, or tree-lines in a park,
we may begin to understand, but find we're in the dark.

Adenosine triphosphate (ATP)
   The molecule that
   stores energy from biochemical reactions and
   supplies energy for biochemical reactions
   in a cell, the "energy molecule."

Carbohydrates
   Energy-producing organic compounds
   of carbon, hydrogen, and water that plants
   use to build the more familiar carbohydrates of food.

Quantum
   Particle of light, photon.

PHOTOSYNTHESIS

For 90 plus three million miles,
Sun's light beams traveled straight,

continued on to chlorophyll,
uncommon photon fate.

With light reactions' energy,
new oxygen in air,

the molecules in cycle Krebs
increased electron share,

producing things like ATP,
near thirty-eight the gain.

This done in respiration with
electron transport chain.

Next step is Calvin cycle dark
to carbohydrates build

and balance out the charges with
electron spaces filled.

The quantum, once a part of sun,
ejected from its place,

became a part of living plant,
"sun" flower sent through space.

Notes

The theory of Punctuated Equilibrium
(or Equilibria) holds that species remain in
equilibrium with their environment for
long stretches of time that are punctuated
by periods of much more rapid change.

66

PUNCTUATED EQUILIBRIA IN LIFE

The change in species past and yet to come
is punctuated equilibrium,
should it occur so relatively fast,
in generations, not in ages vast,
caused by mutations beneficial,
not natural selection gradual,
to cause resulting incremental steps
amid so many stable, lasting reps.

Another case of this scenario
is how relationships of humans grow.
At home most children learn necessities
of eating, drinking, dressing, saying "please."
Next lessons: reading, writing, 'rithmetic,
learned in the home or at a school of brick,
curricula for teaching many sorts:
in music, acting, science, playing sports.

Among the punctuations that we face
are those in which we have to change our place.
As new adults, we leave our parents' home
and to a place of work or study roam.
We look for equilibrium in life,
perchance in role of husband or a wife
then children cause mutations in the plan
as sweetest punctuation in the clan.

As they adapt to changes in their youth
by using wisdom that we've left as truth,
while making thousand choices for their days,
we see their childhood full of "yeas" and "nays."
When children leave, the quiet makes us sad,
there's no one left to call us Mom or Dad.
With children gone, there's nothing left to do,
but learn an art or craft or something new.

My raw knowledge allowed me to identify
the goose without knowing its rarity.

TWO BIRDING CLASSES

I took a weekly birding course, two lectures and two labs.
Attendance most important, so professor kept close tabs

on outdoor labs with early start at February's close.
Once went to look by power plant, where not all water froze.

The wind chill fifty-odd below, we mostly just saw fog,
some mallards and black duck or two that shivered on a log.

Objective lenses of binocs and their eyepieces, too,
were frosted like my spectacles, which ruinates their view.

We found ourselves, just one month on, in warmer birding park,
the temp'rature was fifty then, *above* the zero mark.

Eleven species waterfowl plus other water birds.
I first saw rarest of them all, but didn't say the words

for I knew not the rarity white-fronted goose I saw
was for the teachers of the course, whose knowledge was not raw.

Goose Pond produced more birds that day, enough to whet our thirst
for seeing rare and migrant birds, like goose that I saw first.

Notes

Flotsam

Wreckage from a ship or other craft.

Jetsam

Material thrown from a ship or other craft.

RIVER

As River passes 'fore our
eyes, in-finite water that we see
will grow in its apparent size
to hold the next infinity.

So many times is water drawn
from where it comes to where it goes,
replenishing from dawn till dawn,
the water of the river flows,

flows over ev'ry substrate stone,
each form of Life on riverbed,
and those that river's current meet,
where freely-swimming fish are fed.

If flotsam, jetsam do abound,
infinity of here declines,
where everlasting now is found,
we must build ecologic shrines.

Index

Image prepared by Edie McBain

About the Author

The scientifically romantic nature poetry of Paul Košir has its academic roots in his nine years as a student at the University of Wisconsin-Madison. There he earned bachelor's degrees in math, natural science, and history. In 2010 he received a master's degree in natural resources and environmental education from UW-Stevens Point.

The experiential poetry was drawn mostly from his twelve years as the naturalist at Wyalusing State Park near Prairie du Chien, Wisconsin. He also drew on this background to write articles for *Wisconsin Natural Resources* and *La Crosse Magazine* and to publish the book, Wyalusing History.

Košir has taught biology, physical science, and math at the high school level and earth science, biology, and environmental issues at the college level. As a naturalist, he taught all ages about nature through hikes, programs, and displays, something he still does occasionally as a volunteer.

Born in Milwaukee, Košir now lives in La Crosse with his wife and their two sons. He enjoys writing, hiking, bird-watching, gardening, traveling, and visiting relatives.

Other books by Paul Košir:

Perspectives of Nature

Perspectives of Nature:
Volume 2

Perspectives of Nature:
Volume 3